# Magnetic

**Also** by Alexandra Vasiliu

*Dare to Let Go*

*Healing Is a Gift*

*Be My Moon*

*Healing Words*

*Blooming*

*Time to Heal*

*Through the Heart's Eyes*

*Plant Hope*

# Magnetic
## A Poetry Collection for Lovers

Alexandra Vasiliu

Stairway Books
2021

For permission requests, please contact Alexandra Vasiliu at
Stairway Books, 3324 E Ray Rd #1228, Higley, AZ 85236, or at
alexandra@alexandravasiliu.net

*Magnetic: A Poetry Collection for Lovers* by Alexandra Vasiliu.
Stairway Books, 2021
ISBN-13: 9798516712920

First edition, September 2021

Editing services provided by Chris at www.hiddengemsbooks.com
Cover Illustrations: Nataletado via www.shutterstock.com
Illustrations: Singleline via www.shutterstock.com

*To all those who believe
in the magnetic force of love*

# Contents

# Magnetic

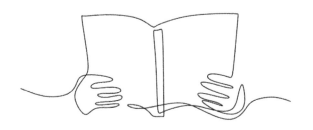

## Whenever I Miss You

Whenever I miss you,
I start writing
love poems
to your beautiful heart.

I tell you everything
about my feelings
and dreams.

I imbue every word
with all my hopes.

I blow wishes for us
into the sky.

I embellish the world
with my emotions
and create poetry
around you.
Is there a better way
to tell you
how much I love you?

Whenever I miss you,
my soul yearns
to capture in writing
all my feelings
for you.

I send you love poems
on delicate zephyrs
and hope
that every light breeze
will stir your heart
with my emotions.
Is there a better way
to tell you
how much I miss you?

Regardless of the time,
whether 3:00 a.m. or 5:00 p.m.,
I never stop writing
love poems
to your beautiful heart.
I miss you.
Is there a better way
to tell you
how much I want you
to be with me?

Every day,
I spill my secrets through poetry
and pray,

"Oh, God,
please help my beloved read
all my poems
with the eyes of his heart.
Allow him to feel
the poetry of my soul.
I don't want
to find my letters
undelivered and marked,
*Return to sender.*
Please make it
so he does not
brush off my feelings.
My love is knocking at his door."
Is there a better way
to tell you
how much I want you to stay?

If you read my poems,
I hope you will ask
for more love
to appear at your heart's door.

## Come

I would like you
to lie down beside me.
Please,
come close to me,
so close
you can enter my chest,

open the door to my heart,
share a dance with my emotions,
and introduce yourself
to my dreams.
I am waiting for you.

## Longing Is a Special Sense

How beautiful love is—
though we are apart
and vast lands divide us,
we can still hear
each other's sighs of longing.

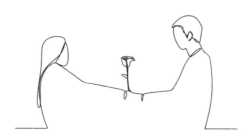

This is how I tell you,
"I miss you, darling."

This is how you answer,
"I miss you too."

## The Only Wealth

I swear,
if our love had not existed,
I would have been
the poorest woman
in the world.
I would have never discovered
my heart
overflowing
with poetry
and beauty.
I would have never found
my inner reservoirs
of sensitivity,
generosity,
acceptance,
and understanding.

I would have never tasted
the simplicity of happiness
when all I had
was just a handful of kind words.

If our love had not existed,
I would have never been able
to touch the sky
with my bare hands.

I would have never felt
that spring can also come
from your loving heart,
bringing so much hope and happiness.
I would have never known
how much joy you radiate
or how much strength exists
inside me.

If our love had not existed,
I would have been
the poorest woman
in the world.

## Speak to Me

My love,
let your heart become fluent
in kindness.

Speak to me with love
and tenderness.
Surround me
with light
and joy.
This is the only way
you will wake up
my slumbering heart.
This is the only way
we will both feel alive.

## No Matter the Distance

Don't cry, my love.
I will be back.
I know it is going to be hard,
for yearning has never been easy,
but I will return to you.

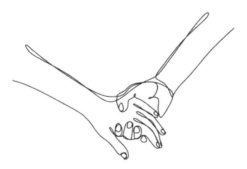

No matter the distance,
I will feel your love
calling me back.

Wait for me
with poetry
beneath your skin
and the elixir of life
on your lips.

No matter the distance,
I will always come back.

## Only a Mirror

I miss you so much
that even if I shattered
all the mirrors
in this world,
I would still see your face,
reflected
deep down
within my heart.

## If You Miss Me

If you miss me,
close your eyes,
imagine kissing me
and relive all the fleeting moments
that we've shared together.

Let your love flow over my face.
Let your feelings water my heart.
Let hope spring up in your soul.
There is no way
I could not return to you.

## We Hit It Off

Last night,
you opened
the window of your heart
and called to me,
"My love!
My love!"

The whole world
was engulfed
by the beauty
of your heart.

Last night,
I heard your call
and followed
your silken voice.

I opened the window
of my heart and
flew on the wings
of longing
all the way
to you.

Last night,
two galaxies collided
and created
a new world
of softness
and poetry.

## Your Little Pearl

You took my hands
in yours
and said,
"Could you protect my heart?
In return, I will give you
my little pearl."

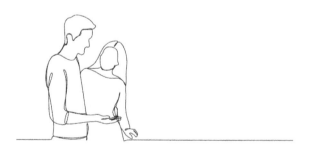

I felt so anxious.
How could I carry
your tiny treasure
without breaking it
or hurting you?
I sighed
and prayed to God,
"Please empower me
to love him beautifully
and embrace him
with ardent emotions.
Help me unlock my inner strength,
so I can give him
all my powerful feelings
and wrap him
in a blissful, intense love.
Please, God, help me
love him in such a pure way
that we can endlessly deepen
our connection,
treasure each other,
celebrate our emotional wellness,
and never hurt one another."

Then I looked straight into your eyes
and told you,

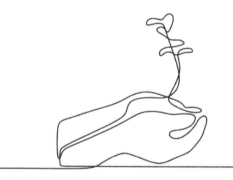

"In the name of love,
I promise
I will hold your heart close
as I would bear a baby
in my womb.
I will protect
your little treasure
inside my heart's shell
as I would cherish
a new life.
I might not be perfect
in my efforts,

"I might not have everything
all figured out,
yet I will be honest
in my love for you.
I will do everything
in my power
to never hurt you.
My darling,
give me your love,
your whole heart now.
I promise
I will always take care
of your little pearl."

# Hunger

Do you ever feel
my vibrant,
passionate heart
searching the world for you?
Do you ever feel
how much I want you
close to me?
Do you ever feel my longing
when I am howling at the moon?
Do you ever feel my heart
looking for you
under the bedsheets
at 3:00 a.m.?
Do you ever feel my hunger?
You are my ambrosia.

# In the Morning

Early in the morning,
I wrap myself in your whispers,
dive into your heart,
and soak up all your love.
I melt into your kisses
and rise from your arms anew.
I am your dawn.
Your sun.
Your light.
Isn't this
what you have always wanted
for me?

## Love Songs for You

Beneath my skin,
deep down in my heart,
plays my song of longing for you.
Can you hear my heart's trills?
Can you hear my love craving you?
Please embrace me now.
Only you will set me free
from this sweet heartache.

# Happy

When I fell for you,
I made a secret promise—
not to lose myself in loving you.

And as if you heard it,
you helped me
keep my promise.

You made me discover
new parts of my soul
whose existence I was unaware of.

You built love dreams with me
and helped me gain confidence
in my poetic heart.

You helped me
stop childish habits
and grow
into a better version of myself.

You made me feel
like I could hold
the sky.

You renewed
my faith in love.

How can I ever thank you
for encouraging me
to find my way in love?
How can I ever thank you
for making me feel alive and whole?
How can I ever thank you
for opening my heart's eyes?
How can I ever thank you
for showing me
love is all about
healing,
growth,
peace,
and happiness?

Falling in love with you
was the beginning of
something truly perfect.

My darling,
I love you beyond measure.
Please accept my heart
as an everlasting gift.
You helped me
find my true self
through love.

## Your Promise

I will be the sun of joy over you,
bringing light to you
and scattering
the rays of my love
over your heart.

I will make you happy
effortlessly.
You are my spring,
my joy,
my magic,
my passion,
my purpose,
my miracle,
my heart.
You are my universe.

## My Regret

I love you
with all my heart
and all the strength
of my dreams.
That is why
I will carry to the grave
only a single regret:
not to have met you earlier.

## Gifts

I wish
I could build
a peaceful world for you.
I would face any storm
to live with you there
for innumerable hours.
I would love you even more.

I wish
I could use magic
and whisk you away
to the beautiful *Lands Of Forever*.
I would listen to
your fantastical stories
and love you even more.

I wish
I could tuck all my love
inside your chest
and let you feel my emotions.
I would give you every dream I have
and love you even more.

I wish
I could do all the impossible things
and be everything you want me
to be:
a poem writtcn in hope,
a woman changing through art,
a moon shining bright,
an ocean endlessly returning to shore.
I know
I would love you even more.
So much more.

I wish
I could be your destiny.
I would love you even more,
so much more.

## Let My Love Follow You

Wherever you go,
my love will follow you.
Like the earth orbits the sun.
Like the moon chases the darkness.
Like the night shadows the day.
My love will follow you
with unwavering devotion.

I will never complain
about being separated by either
time or great distances.
Wherever you go,
the invisible threads connecting
our hearts
will always keep us tethered together.

Wherever you go,
my heart will instantly get up
and follow at your side.

I will never get tired
of loving you.
I will always dare to love you more.
I will never have enough of you.

Wherever you go,
my heart is ready
and in it for the long haul.

Wherever you go,
my heart will follow faithfully,
for home is where you find
your heart.

Wherever you are, my love,
wherever you go,
I will be right behind you,
like the sky frames the sun.
My love will always carry you.
My love will always follow you.

## Your Love Is a Flower

Stop buying me roses.
They always fade
and eventually wither.

Dare to love me
and make me your flower.

Dare to make me bloom
and let our hearts intertwine
like wildflowers
in a sunny field.

In love,
I never fade or wither,
just as perennial flowers always
remain alive
in their roots.
I never lose my spirit.

I never lose my hope.
I never lose my innocence.
The petals of my heart's flower
never wilt or fall.

In love,
I always grow and bloom
as sunflowers always thrive
with sunshine and warmth.

## With Your Eyes

Could you kiss me
with your eyes?
Poems would blossom
in my heart
and make me say,
*I love you too.*

## Not Everything Is Visible

The world is made
of so much more
than the physical and material.
Such as feelings.
My feelings for you,
and your feelings for me.

Have I ever thanked you
for building our home
with beautiful feelings?
Thank you, my darling,
for making our home
out of love.

## So Worth Waiting For

I was willing to wait
as long as it takes
for a love
that could be better
than any dream.
I was willing to wait for a love
that could be a lighthouse
amid storm-wracked seas.
I was willing to wait for a love
so strong
that I could build my life on it.

And when I met you,
I saw a promise
in your heart.

It read:
"And they lived happily ever after."
I didn't need any other proof
to believe in you,
because I felt
that you brought me
the love
I was waiting for.
Since then,
we have walked hand in hand
through all kinds of storms,
yet it felt like
there was only light shining
around us.
You were so worth waiting for.

## The Big Day

I often think about
the day
you told me,
"Let's erase one word
from our language.
Let's forget *heartbreak*.
Never use it.
Never whisper it.
Never think about it.
Let's expel it from our hearts."

"Let's do so,"
I said.
"We will share a love
where neither you or I
will ever feel hurt or alone."

On that day
spring emerged
from our thoughts
and we started to believe
in love.

Nothing is impossible for two souls
in love.

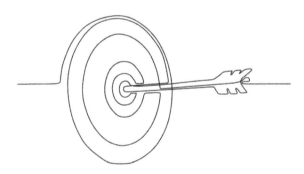

## The Flow of Time

When I wanted to stop time,
I was surprised to see you smiling.
"Put your ear
against my chest
and listen to my heart,"
you told me.

"Can you hear?
There is no ticking of the clock.
Joy covers everything.
Whenever you are around me,
my heart explodes with love.
Don't think about time.
We are finally together.
We are made to celebrate
our pure love.
Can you believe that?
There is nothing more important.
Put your heart
against my chest,
and love me.
I will do the same.
I will love you
with all my heart,
with all my strengths and hopes.
I will love you
until we can no longer hear
any ticking of the clock.
I will love you
until we forget
the flow of time.

"I will love you
until joy will be the name
we give to our lives.
I will love you
until time stops.
Put your ear
against my chest
and listen to my heart.
Joy covers everything."

## Together

You were running to me
from light-years away.

I was dreaming of you
with the speed of light.

We had loved one another
long before we met.

## Hand in Hand

My darling,
don't keep your hands
in your pockets
while we take a walk.
Hold my hand, please.
I want to feel your warmth.
Hands are meant for conveying
all the secret words
locked up tight
inside our hearts.
Take my hand
like you would cradle
a part of my soul.

## Be Patient

Please, stay with me.
Be patient.
Don't go away;
I am rebuilding myself.

I know that growth takes time,
but in the end,
I will give you
the most precious part of me.

Wait and pray for us, my love.
My heart is struggling
to become your home.

Alexandra Vasiliu

## Intimacy

When you get closer to me,
you will see
all that I hide inside my heart.

You will see my dreams
and this will be
the most revelatory discovery
you can make about me.

One day,
you will see all my feelings
and feel more connected to me,
for intimacy requires two bare souls
always standing in love and light.

## Togetherness

Please, darling,
walk with me
through the storms
of this life.
Hand in hand is the recipe
for a life
in which neither you
nor I
will lose our way.

## Your Kisses

When you first touched my lips,
you made me feel
like I had finally found my home.

"I am going to write a poem
on your lips,"
you told me.

And I felt like
I was made of stardust and magic.

"This poem is about *you*,"
you said and kissed me more.

I held my breath
and wanted
to keep that fleeting moment forever.

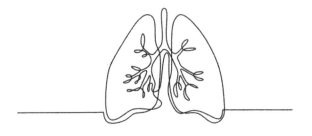

Grace poured out from my heart.

"From this day on,
my world equals *you*,
for you are my poem,
my art,"
you said
and kissed me again.

All the words faded.
Only the two of us were
in this world,
with an indigo sky above,
so much poetry around us,
and a raging wildfire
within our hearts.

## I Am Here

You whispered in my ear,
"I am here
to heal your heart's wounds
through love.

I am here
to love you
and set the seal of my devotion
on your heart.
Shh! Don't say anything.
Let *Joy*
be the name
of your heart.
I am here
to make you happy."

Alexandra Vasiliu

## So Close

At 3:00 a.m.,
I always wish
to enter your heart,
see your emotions,
and get to know
your beautiful feelings.
At 3:00 a.m.,
I always look inside your heart
for a cozy place,
one where I could dwell
with my dreams
for eternity.

## Whenever We Meet

Whenever we meet,
you seed flowers
in my heart.

Each time,
you promise me
that one day,
I will have a garden
full of beautiful emotions.
Nevertheless, I always wonder,
"Will you stay with me
to make my flowers grow?"

## I Still Remember

Although I've forgotten your words
from our first date,
I still remember
how you made my heart soar
toward the sky,
and the way you softly grabbed
my hand
then held it in yours.
The rest of the world
diminished to the size of
a sunflower seed.

## Not a Burden

I will carry the magic
of your love
everywhere.
I will shelter it
deep down in my heart
and treasure it eternally.
Together we'll float,
rising above worldly worries
while I protect it
from all life's trials.
I promise
I will carry your love
in my heart,
like a second heart containing
my essence,
my little paradise.

## The Most Beautiful Dress

When you touch me,
it feels like
you dress me up
with the most beautiful gown
in the whole world.
A gown cut from
the fabrics of
tenderness and love.
A gown made of
your passionate feelings for me.
You dress me up
making sure
that every inch
of my body
and soul
are covered

with your longing
and sensuality.
How could I ever wish
to put ordinary clothes on me again?

Your love outshines
all other dresses
no matter how fancy or sophisticated.

My darling,
dress me up
in your love.
Cover me
with your affection.
I want to find myself
glowing from within,
beneath the layers of my skin.
I want to see myself
beautiful and precious
through your eyes
that truly love me.

## With Your Hand

I will always hold your hand
in mine.

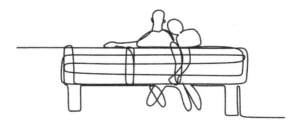

You are the only one
worthy of
being loved and cherished.
You are the only one
worthy of
wearing my love like a crown.
You are the only one
worthy of
ruling as the king of my heart.
You. No one else.

## Only You

Only you can heal,
love,
and refine me
at the same time.
There is no in-between.
And that is why
I fall for you repeatedly,
every second
feeling like
it is the first time.

## How I Have Lived

Somewhere between
*I love you*,
and *I will never leave you*,
there is a space.

A tiny space
where I have always prayed for us,

"Oh, God, please
give me the wisdom
to love my man
with fidelity
and strength.
Oh, God, please
teach me
the art of devotion,

so that I can always show him
my undivided love."

Somewhere between
*I love you,*
and *I will never leave you,*
there is a space
where I have lived
my whole life
praying for us.

# If I Could Describe Happiness

If I could describe happiness to you,
I would never limit myself
to words.
I would paint
rivers of love
flowing
from my heart to yours.
And I would give my love
sailboats
formed from longing
to quickly navigate
back and forth
from my heart
to yours.
But I would never limit myself
to words.

I would swim
into love
every day,
and you will be heartened
when you taste
all the little miracles
of my strength and femininity.
But I would never limit myself
to words.

I would help you get lost
in my secret depths
every night
and emerge with stars
in your eyes.
But I would never limit myself
to words.

If I could describe happiness
to you,
I would speak in
the language of angels.
And I promise,
I would never ever limit myself
to earthly words.

Alexandra Vasiliu

## I Will Never Forget You

I will never forget you,
I promise.
Only you can kiss me
with your eyes.
Only you can hug me
with the arms of your heart.

Only you can reveal
my dreams
with your lips.
Only you can dress me up
with your joy.
I will never forget you,
I promise.
The way
you surround me with love
feels so perfect—
as if you have stolen
this happiness
from paradise
especially for me.
I will never forget you,
I promise.

## Like a Desert

In your arms,
I feel
like an arid desert
after the deluge of a warm rain.

## All the Poems of My Heart

If you love me,
open my heart's book
and read my inner poems.
Letter by letter,
word by word,
emotion by emotion,
feeling by feeling.

I am offering you my heart.
Read my poetry, please.
I am standing here,
in front of you,
vulnerable
and devoted
at the same time.
I hope
this is the way
we can feel more connected
than ever before.
Open my heart's book
and read
my inner,
perfect,
crazy poems.

## You and I

Even when we are in a crowded place,
I don't see other faces than yours.
It is like we are
the only two living souls
on this earth.
You live
only in my eyes,
and I smile
only for your gaze.
There is no room for others.
The world is ours,
and together we make
a complete existence.

## Being with You

Promise me
we will never get lost.
We have each other
and the whole sky to claim as ours.
Promise me
we will hold hands forever.
It will be such bliss
to walk with you in life,
knowing
that love is our only reality.

## I Wish

I still wish
we could open the door of time
and return to the place
where we first met.

I imagine
we would become young
and fall in love all over again.
I imagine
we could hold the flames of passion
with our bare hands.

Alexandra Vasiliu

We could dance
around the moon
every night
and beckon magic upon us
until dawn.
I imagine
we could get lost
in a labyrinth of whispered words
and abandon our lunacy
in an everlasting kiss.
I imagine
we could spend our whole life
together and in love.
Nothing else.
And that would be everything.
I still wish
we could return
to the place where we first met.
Don't you also wish to relive
our happiness
all over again?
Let's open the door of time.

## You Are the Sun

Have I ever told you
how precious
and unique you are?
Whenever you look at me,
I can feel the sun
rising
from my heart.

## In Your Arms

Let's dance
like the moon and the sun.

Looking in each other's eyes,
we will move rhythmically,
spreading grace
and light
around us.

We will be free and untamed
in our dance,
twisting and swirling
until we collide
and burst into thousands of galaxies
made of love.

We will embrace one another
without physical bodies.

Our hearts never needed form
to feel deliriously happy.

We will be the moon and the sun
chasing each other
and discovering
what magnetism is all about.

Our intricate dance
might not be
perfect,
but I promise
to make sure
we will never forget it.

Let's dance, my love,
and make memories
worth remembering.

There is so much beauty in love.

## Seeding

Whenever your lips touch mine,
you seed
thousands of flowers
beneath my skin.
You sow passion in my flesh
and help my fire come out
from my heart.

"You turn my body into a garden
and my heart into a hurricane,"
I told you.

"I am so happy I did.
You smell like happiness now."

## I Was Made for You

I am your missing rib;
I fit perfectly
in your arms,
so please, stay.
I was born for you.

## Unchanged

"Look up at the sky,"
you told me.

"The universe is infinite,
the sun is beautiful every day,
the bold stars shine bright
every evening.
Everything speaks to us
about staying unchanged
and remaining timeless.
Let my heart tell you the same truth.
My love for you is forever."

## Let Me Touch You

My darling,
let me touch you
where you feel vulnerable.
My heart has invisible hands
that can reach you
even
at your most profound depths.

Let me touch you with love.
This is the only way I can tell you
how much I care about you.
I will hold your soul
in my arms
as I would keep a little piece
of heaven.
I will never break it.
I will never let it slip
through my fingers.
I will treasure it
with love.
My darling,
let me touch you
where hands are of no use.
This is the only way
I will never let you go.

## Hopes and Dreams

How could I ever feel sad
since my heart is a fertile womb
filled with hopes
and dreams?
All these unborn babies kick
and squirm
within my heart.
All these babies are so eager
to have a life
worth fighting for.
I am a happy mother-to-be
for so many hopes and dreams.
Put your hand
on my womb of emotions,
touch my heart,
and feel

my tender parts
growing
for you.
My heart is filled
with hopes and dreams—
for you,
for me,
for us.

# Home

Hold me close in your heart;
it has been forever
since I first learned
what a warm home means.

## Put My Heart into Words

Sometimes,
when I feel my heart
as wide,
open,
and beautiful
as the sky,
I wonder
how I can put
what I'm feeling into words.
Can the sky truly be captured?
Can my love for you
be immortalized
in poetry?

## Traces of Poetry

I hope
one day,
you will find me.

I leave
traces of poetry
in every simple little thing
I touch.

## You Are Easy to Be Loved

Nothing is difficult or complicated
with you.
You are easy to love.
You make everything so simple.
And this is why I am so happy with
you.
Your magic turns everything
into possible things.
Isn't this the poetry of your soul?

## Looking at Your Face

At dawn,
when light begins to pour in
through the windows,
I love looking at your face.
Closed eyes.
Sleeping heart.
And so much love
eager to burst through your lips.
You are a bud
waiting to grow
and bloom.
I just want to be your fragrance.
To me,
this is what poetry is all about.

## Waiting

Waiting for someone
as freethinking as you
has always been
a form of freedom.

Without labels or pressure,
free of society's constraints,
I have waited for you
on the porch
of my heart,
scanning the horizon
and staring at the roads
for hours.

I have waited for you
with unwavering loyalty.

I have never felt disappointed.
I truly believed
that one day,
you would show up
with heaven in your heart
and flowers of hope
in your eyes.
And one day,
you did.

Waiting for you
has always been
a form of freedom.

## So Much Beauty

I've got
savage fires under my skin,
hidden oceans in my heart,
and hundreds of galaxies
entangled throughout my hair.
I've got
so much beauty
craving your touch.
I've got
so much wild purity
aching for you.
When you meet me,
please stay forever.

## You Are a Love Poem

"I don't know
how it is humanly possible,"
you told me,
"but let me tell you,
darling,
you are a love poem
in the body of a woman.

Sometimes,
I pinch myself
fearing this is just a dream.

Yet here you are
standing in front of me,
so beautiful,
smiling

and carrying your soul
as you would wear
a golden crown.

"You run your fingers
through your long hair
while talking
and laughing.
I am hypnotized by you.
I don't know
how it is humanly possible,
but you are so rare,
wild,
and wonderful
in the way that
only a love poem can be.

Nevertheless,
when the sunrays enter this magic
and dress you up
with brightness,
I look at you
in even more awe.
I am entranced.
Are you from this world?
I snap my fingers,
yet you are still here
in front of me.
I see your naked soul;
so pure,
tender,
beautiful,
soft,
and strong.
You are a poem
from head to toe,
and from the inside out.
When I look at you,
I feel the urge
to change myself into someone
as gorgeous as you.

I am so lucky
to see you like this.
A poem.
A love poem
in the body of a woman.
Darling,
to me,
you are everything
I dream
about poetry."

I touched your lips
and said,
"Shh!
Don't tell anyone.
I am truly made of love,
poetry,
and softness.
But hide this secret
in your heart.
I want to stay invisible
and rare
in this world.
I want to kiss you

and be kissed.
"I want to love you and be loved.
I want to hide in your arms
and get lost inside your heart.
Nothing less.
Nothing else.
Strip away all my poetry layers,
and you will see
there is a woman within,
waiting to be loved like a queen.

"For you,
I want to be everything
you dream and don't dream.
Dare to hug me.
I am your woman in love."

## Like a Magnet

If it is true
that at some point in our lives
we become our thoughts,
then I want to become
a beautiful, bright, bold thought
dedicated to you.
On that day,
there will be only one person
in my mind
and that person will be you.
No one else.
From that day on,
I will fall for you incessantly.
You will forever be on my mind.
Nothing else.

If it is also true
that at some point in our lives
we become our feelings,
then I want to become
a fresh, fabulous, fierce feeling
dedicated to you.
On that day,
there will be only one person
in my heart
and that person will be you.
No one else.
From that day on,
I will fall for you every moment.
You will forever be
my whole heart.
Nothing else.

If it is true
that at some point in our lives
we become what we love,
then I want to become
everything that I love about you.
Nothing else.
I will reflect

what I cherish about you
and mirror
your loving heart.
From that day on,
you will always radiate
from my inner self.
From that day on,
there will be only one person
in my mind and heart:
you.
From that day on,
our souls will be one,
infusing each other
with love and peace.

## If You Leave Me

If you leave me,
I will listen to your footsteps
moving farther
and farther from me.

I will count
all my fading dreams
of our happiness
while you descend the steps outside.
*One, two, three, four*
until I get to *one million.*
When I stop counting,
I will wonder
how you could ever live
so far from me.
You can't.
I know it.
And you can't feel alive
without me either.
This is why
I will fill the night sky
with my dreams for us.
I know
that when you look up,
you will see all the sparkling stars
whispering your name
as I used to do.
I hope
that one day,

you will come back to me,
for you can never erase
the memory of our love
from your heart.

If you leave me,
I will build a safe road
for you.
A road through the sky
all the way back to me.
For I understand
you will need to know
the universe
of my heart,
my whole poetry,
to return to me
and start over again.
Even if you leave me,
I know
you will still think of me,
for our hearts will always be
two strong magnets
attracting each other.

## Magnetic

"You are so magnetic,
you can pull even the distant sun
toward you,"
you told me.

I looked into a mirror.
I saw a light
scintillating
in my heart,
a radiant force
of love
bursting
from my soul,
a glowing allure
around my body,
a refreshing luminosity
on my face,
an irresistible desire
to be closer to you.
A captivating energy flowed
from inside out.

You were right.
I was magnetic.

But when I looked into your eyes,
I saw my heart
reflected so naturally
in you.

"I am magnetic,
my dear,
for you are magnetic too.
We mirror each other perfectly,
for we are
two beautiful, bold souls
living on the orbit of love."

## Dear Reader,

Thank you very much for reading my poetry collection.

I hope that my poems helped you discover your unique, magnetic beauty and renewed your faith in love and happiness.

If so, please take a moment and show your appreciation by writing a short review on the website where you purchased this book.

Your support means a lot to me. Thank you very much, beautiful soul.

With love and poetry,
Alexandra

# About the Author

Alexandra Vasiliu is an inspirational poet, and the bestselling author of *Healing Is a Gift, Healing Words, Time to Heal, Dare to Let Go, Be My Moon, Blooming, Through the Heart's Eyes*, and *Plant Hope*. Her poetry touches thousands of people, one heart at a time.

As an award-winning poet, she uses her imagination to write books that help people overcome life's adversities, heal their emotional wounds, increase empathy, find hope and inner peace, become stronger, and love again.

Alexandra double majored in Literature and French for her undergraduate degree before pursuing her Ph.D. in Medieval Literature.

When she isn't busy writing, she can be found browsing in libraries and bookstores, outdoors chasing violet sunsets, exploring pine woods, or spending time with her family at the beach.

Get in touch with her on Instagram @alexandravasiliupoetry and Facebook @AlexandraVasiliuWriter. Or visit her at alexandravasiliu.net. She loves hearing from her readers.

Made in the USA
Las Vegas, NV
27 December 2023